Botanical Dyes on Wood

REBECCA DESNOS

Botanical Dyes on Wood

Published in 2021 by Rebecca Desnos
www.rebeccadesnos.com

First Edition

Copyright © Rebecca Desnos 2021.

First published in 2018 as an eBook.

All rights reserved. No part of this publication may be reproduced, stored in a retrieval system, or transmitted in any form or by any means without written permission of the publisher.

The information in this book is true and complete to the best of the author's knowledge. All recommendations are made without guarantee. The author has made every effort to ensure that all instructions given in this book are accurate and safe, but cannot accept liability, whether direct or consequential, however arising.

ISBN: 978-0-9955566-9-0 (paperback)
ISBN: 978-0-9955566-3-8 (eBook)

All photography is by Rebecca Desnos, except the portraits on pages 4 and 94 which are by *siobhancalder.com*

Hi! I'm Rebecca Desnos—a natural dyer in the UK, a writer, mother, and an all-round plant lover.

I'm passionate about making colours from local plants and showing others how they can do the same!

My first book *Botanical Colour at your Fingertips* (2016) will show you my method for dyeing fabric and yarn. My latest magazine is *Plant Dye Zine* (2020) and it's full of botanical dye projects.

Welcome

Thanks for purchasing this book all about dyeing wood with plants.

Within the next 90 or so pages, I will show you my entire method for dyeing wood, which I've been using for many years. I'll also share techniques for painting wood so you can make patterns and also apply dye to larger pieces of wood. The possibilities for painting and dyeing wood are truly endless.

Some of the principles in this guide have been adapted from my first natural dyeing book, *Botanical Colour at your Fingertips*. Dyeing wood is similar to fabric in many ways – it's a natural evolution of ideas. Everything I show you in this book is just a starting point, so don't feel limited by what I create. Let your imagination take you on a new journey!

I hope you enjoy this book and have fun with these ideas. I'd love it if you shared your results on Instagram and used the hashtag #rebeccadesnos so I can see what you've created!

~ Rebecca

P.S. There are lots more dye tutorials on my blog: **rebeccadesnos.com**

Contents

Section 1	**Introduction**	9
	Getting started	11
	Dyeing v.s. staining	12
	My approach to dyeing	15
	Safety	20
	Equipment	23
	Selecting wood to dye	25
Section 2	**Preparing the dye**	29
	Dyeing with whole plants	31
	Choosing dye plants	32
	Colours	34
	Let's make our dye	37
	Darkening dyes with iron water	40
	Storing dye	42
Section 3	**Dyeing beads, buttons & small objects**	45
	Pretreating wood with soya milk	46
	Dyeing wood in a dye bath	53
	Using iron to darken dyes	59

Section 4	**Painting dye with a brush**	61
	Painting flat surfaces	62
	Painting round beads	65
	Painting furniture	66
Section 5	**Aftercare**	69
	Oiling wood	71
	Other sealants	72
	Colour fastness	75
Section 6	**Appendix**	79
	Painting paper & fabric	81
	Pretreating fabric in soya milk	84
	Hammering flowers onto wood	86
	Glossary	88
	UK - US vocabulary differences	90
	Bibliography	93
	About Rebecca Desnos	95
	Enjoy your dyeing!	97

Section 1

Introduction

- Getting started
- Dyeing v.s. staining
- My approach to dyeing
- Safety
- Equipment
- Selecting wood to dye

BOTANICAL DYES ON WOOD

Getting started

If you dye fabric and stir your pot with a wooden spoon then you are already dyeing wood. The colours on our spoons naturally build up over time. Years ago, it was my collection of colourful wooden spoons that first inspired me to dye beads.

Have you ever noticed that your wooden stirring spoons don't take on as much colour as the fabric in the dye pot? Once a spoon is dry, it's often a paler shade than the dyed fabric. But if we keep using the spoon over and over again it eventually becomes very dark. Wood is very receptive to layers of dye – the dye seeps into deeper parts of the wood and it becomes darker in colour after several sessions in the dye pot.

The natural darkening of our wooden spoons – our dyeing tools – takes time. When dyeing beads, the process can be speeded up by mordanting or pretreating the wood to help it take up more colour in the dye pot. This way we have more control over dyeing the beads (or other wooden items) and don't need to wait as long for the colour to build up.

Observing the way our dyed spoons change colour over time can also give us clues about the longevity of a dye. For example, the pink spoon opposite was dyed with hibiscus flowers and the colour faded after a few months. The yellow spoon dyed with pomegranate skins stayed the same. From this, we can say that hibiscus isn't a good choice for dyeing something to sell, whereas tannin rich pomegranate skins offer a long-lasting colour that can withstand exposure to light. This is an important factor when dyeing jewellery or other wooden decorative items.

Differences between dyeing & staining

A dye permeates into the deeper layers of the wood, whereas a stain sits on the surface (usually within an oil based medium). A dye is a translucent wash of colour and the wood grain is still visible. Dyes soak into the wood and can enhance the pattern of timber grains. Stains, on the other hand, do not penetrate into the wood.

Stains are used for external timber fencing as they are extremely long-lasting. After lots of exposure to water, the stain eventually begins to peel away from the wood as the oil base can no longer keep it adhered to the surface. Dyes are less colourfast than stains, but for the purposes of making jewellery and dyeing other small indoor decorative items or even furniture, dyes offer a good degree of colour fastness.

When dyeing, we need to be mindful that wood swells up in water and if it gets too wet, the grain can open up and spilt. For this reason, it is often better to layer the dyes and build them up with a few sessions in a dye pot, or even a few applications with a paint brush. If we leave wood to soak in water for too long then it will swell up too much and become waterlogged, which will be detrimental to the structure of the wood. I recommend working in layers: each layer will darken the colour and the dye will penetrate deeper into the fibres of the wood.

In this book I'll show you my methods for layering dyes on wood and share some projects with you along the way. *Time* is an important factor – we can't rush what we are doing as every step counts. Enjoy your dyeing!

BOTANICAL DYES ON WOOD

My approach to dyeing

Dyeing wood isn't that different to dyeing fabric like cotton, since they both contain cellulose. Cellulose is an organic compound and essentially a plant fibre. All plants contain cellulose in varying amounts.

When dyeing wood or any other cellulose-based fibre with botanical dyes, the material will *generally* benefit from mordanting prior to dyeing. This is because cellulose doesn't have a natural affinity to plant dyes in the same way that animal protein fibres (such as wool or silk) do. Cotton and wood benefit from some help to encourage the plant dye particles to bond with the cellulose molecules.

From our stirring spoons, we may notice that wood does not necessarily require a mordant to develop dark shades. Deep colours can develop slowly over time, and building up colour is a slow process. Without a mordant, the colours still last well, especially if we use tannin rich dyes. In my experience, using a mordant of some kind simply speeds up the dyeing process and gives us more control over our final colours.

When choosing a mordant for wood, we can turn to our fabric and yarn dyeing techniques and adapt ideas. I will share with you my preferred methods which I have successfully tried and tested for several years.

1. Soya milk pretreatment

Just like when I dye fabric, my favourite mordanting method for wood is soya milk*. Pretreating with soya milk works by coating the wood with a diluted layer of soy bean protein, which dries and becomes part of the wood. The soy protein doesn't wash off; it stays within the wood fibres. This provides a good base for dyeing and results in a stronger bond between the fibres and the dyes. In practical terms, this means that the dye particles will attach to the wood quicker and the result will be a darker colour on the wood.

Soya milk pretreatment isn't technically the same as mordanting in the traditional sense, with metallic salts such as alum. The chemistry of how the dye particles attach is different – soya milk is actually a binder and not a chemical mordant – but it still helps dyes adhere to fibres. For simplicity, I sometimes use the word "mordanting" when describing soya milk pretreatment.

Without soya pretreatment, the dyeing process is slower and colours are usually lighter. As with our wooden spoons, which are in their raw state, untreated beads require many layers of dye to build up colour. Sometimes we may be looking for a light wash of colour, in which case omitting the soya milk stage is fine and gives us the result we are looking for. I often dye mixed batches of beads – half with a coating of soya milk and half without. If we dye them in the same dye pot, then half will end up darker and half lighter, but they will have the same colour. It's a simple method for creating necklaces with a selection of tones. If we string these beads with some undyed beads, then we conveniently have three shades to play with and we've only had to use one dye pot!

2. Pot as mordant

I do most of my fabric and wood dyeing in aluminium pots. In doing so, we can make use of the reactive quality of the metal. This method is called "pot as mordant". When we dye in an aluminium pot, the dye reacts with the metal. Aluminium can assist in the uptake of dyes and help the colours last longer.

The dye pot is a useful tool that you can use, but it is not absolutely essential to use an aluminium pot. As you will see in this book, I tend to use a lot of tannin rich dyes and tannins work as a mordant in their own right.

You can also use iron or copper pots, which not only act as mordants, but also shift the colour of dyes: iron has a darkening effect, and copper can shift colours to yellows or greens.

3. Tannin rich dyes

For the longest-lasting colours on beads, I like to use tannin rich plants. Tannins act as a natural mordant and colours simply last a lot longer than when dyeing with plants without tannins.

Tannins are naturally occurring compounds found in seeds, leaves, bark and fruit. Tannins are usually brown or yellow in colour.

Some examples of tannin rich dyes that I use in this book are black tea (brown), avocado skins (pinky brown on wood), pomegranate skins (yellow), acorns (brown, and grey with iron added), alder cones (golden brown) and eucalyptus leaves (coral, and grey with iron). Many plants contain some degree of tannins and the list goes on and on. Although many tannin rich plants appear to make beiges or browns on wood, the shades are all quite beautiful in their own right and the magic happens when you put different colours together. You'll see that the golden brown from alder cones is different to the brown from tea leaves, and you can create some subtly beautiful colour palettes.

4. Colours that fade

If you use tannin rich dyes, you'll see for yourself that the colour lasts spectacularly well, but in contrast, other dyes such as hibiscus eventually disappear without leaving any trace. As sad as this is, don't let it deter you from experimenting with less colour fast dyes – you might discover something surprising along the way. When dyeing for our own enjoyment, we can still appreciate the colours while they last and also experiment with our seasonal colour palette. Simply unstring your beads and add a new layer of dye in the dye pot.

Once wood has been pretreated in soya milk, the layer of protein will remain and it can be dyed over and over again. If you plan to over dye your beads, it's best not to oil them as the oil will interfere with the absorption of subsequent coats of dye.

INTRODUCTION

Safety

As with any form of dyeing, there are some common sense precautions we should always take.

- Do not use the same pots and utensils for dyeing and cooking.

- Always work with a window open for good airflow.

- Do not eat food whilst dyeing.

- If working in a kitchen, wipe down surfaces thoroughly after dyeing.

- Wear gloves when taking things out of dye pots. Even though the dyes are from plants, they can be irritating to the skin – especially tannins.

- Keep lids on pots to avoid vapour escaping.

- Avoid inhaling fumes when inspecting a dye pot.

- Be careful when lifting the lid off a steaming pot as you could scald your wrist very easily.

- Make sure you have correctly identified the plants you are dyeing with to ensure that they are not toxic.

- If storing dye or oils (used for sealing the wood) in the fridge, ensure that jars are clearly labelled and out of reach of children.

Dyeing for babies & children

It might be tempting to dye nursing necklaces for babies but I would be extremely cautious of this.

First of all, we need to think about the plants we are using (are they safe to ingest?), the type of pot we use (stainless steel is best, as aluminium may infuse into the wood and therefore be unsuitable to put in the mouth), and be mindful of the wood potentially cracking when chewed on and becoming a choking hazard. The wood may have been weakened in the dyeing process by getting saturated and crack more easily than before. Use your own discretion and be careful if dyeing wood for babies.

For older children who no longer put things in their mouths, it can be lovely to dye wooden toys for them to play with. These can be oiled regularly to nourish the wood and help prevent any cracking.

Equipment

Very little equipment is needed and you will probably have these items if you dye fabric, or you can repurpose old pots and bowls from your kitchen cupboards. Once you've used any of these tools for dyeing, never use them for food again. It can be helpful to put a piece of masking or electrical tape around saucepan and sieve handles to make sure you don't accidentally muddle them up with your kitchen equipment.

These are my essentials:

- A couple of small dye pots/saucepans – ideally aluminium for extra mordanting benefit, but it's not essential if you use tannin rich dyes. I tend to use both stainless steel and aluminium.
- Stainless steel or glass bowls
- Stirring spoons
- Stainless steel sieve: if it's an old sieve make sure it's not rusty as the beads will develop dark spots when they come into contact with it (the dye reacts with iron and darkens in colour).
- Muslin cloths
- Glass jars
- Paintbrushes
- ... and of course a heat source.

BOTANICAL DYES ON WOOD

Selecting wood to dye

Whether you would like to dye beads, buttons, dolls or any other wooden surfaces, there are some things to consider.

1. Unfinished

The wood needs to be untreated and not oiled. We need a porous surface for the dye to attach to the fibres. If you would like to paint furniture with dyes, sand off any varnish or oil to leave a porous surface.

2. Pale colour

For subtle dye colours to show up on wood, it's best to use light coloured timber.

3. FSC certified

Try to source FSC certified wood wherever possible. FSC stands for 'Forest Stewardship Council'. The FSC runs a global forest certification system that allows us to identify, purchase and use wood, paper and other forest products produced from responsibly-managed forests.

4. Hand carved + local

Why not learn to carve your own buttons and beads? Give fallen branches a new lease of life in your beautiful creations. There's a simple tutorial on my blog for carving beads from elder branches. Go to *rebeccadesnos. com/pages/bead-carving*. All you need is a tool for pruning, a small sharp knife, kebab skewer and of course an elder tree. Elder twigs have a soft pith centre which makes them ideal for this project, but you can try with branches from other trees that also have a pith centre.

Alternatively, contact a wood worker and ask them to carve some beads. The beads opposite were made by Lucy from Mopoke Magic (Instagram: *@mopokemagic*). Request pale timber and leave unoiled. This is a lovely way to collaborate with other makers and your beads will be unique!

Carve your own beads from elder twigs: *rebeccadesnos.com/pages/bead-carving*. Photo above by Merlin Fox: *etsy.com/shop/knivesfoxspoons*.

Section 2

Preparing the dye

- Dyeing with whole plants
- Choosing dye plants
- Colours
- Let's make our dye
- Darkening dyes with iron water
- Storing dye

Dyeing with whole plants

When we extract dye from plants, we are essentially making strong tea; we simmer plants in water to coax out the colour. Then the plants are strained out to leave a dye. We must not use too much water in our pot at the beginning – our aim is to make a small volume of concentrated dye liquid. Wood is best dyed in much more concentrated dyes than fabric.

If we dye wood in very diluted dye baths then it will just take much longer to dye the wood to any noticeable colour. We can see this with our wooden spoons – pale dye baths will dye white fabric beautifully, but our wooden spoon won't take on colour at the same rate.

Dyeing wood with homemade dyes is different to dyeing with plant dye extracts in powder form. The first step in our process is to use water to extract the dye from our plants and for this we need to use the minimum amount of water so we end up with concentrated dyes. When dyeing with powdered dyes, we can simply dissolve the powders in a smaller volume of water to begin with (or even add in more powder to increase the concentration). When working with whole plants we need enough water to heat the plants and coax out the colour. It's a matter of experimentation, but always err on the side of caution and don't add in extra water unless your plants are at risk of burning at the bottom of a pot. Less water is usually best. We can of course simmer away any surplus liquid at the end, but aggressive heating can easily brown dyes.

PREPARING THE DYE

Choosing dye plants

Any plants that give colour can be used, but the focus in this book is using tannin rich dyes as they are long lasting and easy to find. The list of potential dye plants you can use is almost endless and depends on the region where you live.

Some of the dye plants used in this book are shown in the photo opposite and you can see on the next page the resulting colours on beads. Here we have eucalyptus leaves, alder cones, acorns, lavender, avocados (for their skins and stones), pomegranates (for their skins) and black tea.

To store plants before dyeing, I like to keep them in paper bags, boxes or cloth bags. The air flow helps keep them dry and prevents mould developing. You can dye with either dry or fresh plants, but you may find a slight difference in the final shade of dye depending on how old the plants are.

Avocado skins and stones freeze well but if you choose to dry them, here are some tips. Try to use the stones before they have darkened. Dried stones usually last for a few months and still give a good colour in the dye pot even when they are a bit wrinkly. Never store dried avocado stones in a sealed container as they will most likely grow mould (yes, this has happened to me!). When you dry avocado skins, try to wash off as much of the green flesh as possible beforehand.

Pomegranate skins dry very well and the colour potential in the skins seems to stay consistent for years.

PREPARING THE DYE

Colours

As we go through the dyeing process, you'll see that I use iron to darken some colours. Eucalyptus dye can look almost blue-like when layered on pale wood, and pink avocado dye can shift to a subtle purple-grey. These tones can really enliven a colour palette by adding depth and contrast.

Don't feel limited by the plants I show you here – the possibilities are endless! Some dyes will inevitably last longer than others and the ones I use in this book are my favourites. Your collection of favourite plants may be different as you have access to other plants. Experiment and test the colourfastness of dyes, which is especially important if you plan to sell any of your work – and have fun!

Never underestimate the power of undyed beads alongside plant dyed beads. The light colour of a pale bead shows the true beauty of the colour next to it. I find that a necklace made up of entirely plant dyed beads can sometimes have a slightly dull effect, but the addition of some undyed beads gives negative space and breathing room to the dyed beads.

What about blue?

You may have noticed that I don't dye with indigo in this book. Wooden beads do in fact dye spectacularly well with indigo and I've used a lot of indigo in the past. The method for dyeing with indigo involves different techniques to the ones within these pages, so indigo dyeing is beyond the scope of this book. But I encourage you to try indigo dyeing – indigo and wood are a perfect match!

Plant dyes

A undyed
B avocado skins
C eucalyptus leaves + iron
D pomegranate skins
E acorns + iron
F alder cones
G coreopsis petals + baking soda
H avocado skins + iron
I lavender leaves
J black tea leaves

PREPARING THE DYE

Let's make our dye

1. Place the dyestuff in an aluminium pot and cover with just enough water so that everything is submerged. Don't use too much water as we are aiming for a concentrated dye – much more concentrated than we would use for dyeing fabric. You don't need a huge volume of dye to dye beads or buttons, so be conservative with the amount of water you add in initially.

2. Heat your pot with the lid on. As a general guide, I suggest heating your plants for one hour, on a low heat, with the aim of coaxing out the colour rather than cooking the plants. Keep a close eye on your pot and top up the water level when the liquid evaporates to avoid burning your dyestuff.

3. Each dyestuff requires different levels of heat and for different durations, to achieve the purest colour. With some plants, you may like to compare continual heat versus soaking in hot water to see which method works best. I tend to use a really low heat to begin with (below simmering point) to see how much colour is extracted. Then I might increase the heat to see if I can extract more colour. It's all a matter of experimentation.

4. After heating your plants, leave them in the pot for a few hours – ideally over night. If you put a small swatch of fabric in the dye pot, then you'll be able to see how the colour develops. Many dyes change colour so be patient and see what happens. If you're using an aluminium pot, this extra time will allow the metal to react with the dye and develop its mordanting effect.

5. When you are happy with your dye colour, strain through a sieve lined with a muslin cloth to remove all the little pieces of the plants. Now your dye is ready.

Dye plant notes

avocados

The skins and stones make a range of pinks, peaches and orange/browns. Wash the green flesh off well and heat gently to keep the dye colour as bright as possible. Leave the dye to oxidise for a few hours and you should get a darker shade. If you don't get pink, try a pinch of bicarbonate of soda to shift the dye colour to alkaline. Add iron to shift the dye to a muted purple/grey.

black tea

Probably the easiest dye plant to find, as lots of us have some in our kitchen cupboard! Make a very strong dye pot of tea with boiling water and allow the leaves to steep to develop a dark colour.

pomegranate skins

The skins of some varieties of pomegranate produce a sunny yellow dye. Dry the skins and store in paper bags – they keep for a long time.

acorns

Acorns are rich in tannins and the dye reacts well with iron to make grey. Store acorns in paper bags or boxes and use through the winter months. Try to collect 'perfect looking' acorns as they are less likely to contain grubs inside. When dyeing with acorns, heat them in water in a dye pot then leave to soak in the dye. The outer shell will split and you can peel it away. Then wearing gloves, you can break the softened acorns apart in your hands. Reheat to extract more dye.

alder cones

Look for these little cones under alder trees throughout the year, especially after rainfall and storms. The cones give their dye generously in the dye pot. They make rich caramel shades – often verging on golden yellow on wood.

eucalyptus leaves

Many colours are possible depending on the variety you use. Keep windows open as the scent can be over-powering. Add iron to darken the dye to a grey, almost black shade. Typically, the more iron you add, the darker the grey.

coreopsis petals

There are many types of coreopsis and the type I have grown is Golden Globe. The petals give their colour very quickly - just pour hot water over the petals. The dye is pH sensitive so add bicarbonate of soda to make orange, and add vinegar to shift to a brighter yellow. The initial vibrance of the colour doesn't remain on wood forever, but a beautifully subtle shade is left.

lavender

The flowers and leaves produce pale browns and sometimes light greys, which can be shifted to darker greys with the addition of iron. Dyeing with lavender is a truly aromatic experience and the scent lingers on the beads for a time afterwards. The soft shade complements many other colours.

Darkening dyes with iron water

Add iron water (also known as rust water) to your dyes to shift the colours and widen your colour palette. Never add iron to your aluminium pots, as it could contaminate all future dye baths (see page 59 for dyeing instructions). Tannin dyes such as acorn dye (shown opposite) react dramatically with iron and the dyes produce various shades of grey. The undertone of the original dye will still show. For example pink avocado dye turns a grey/purple.

I like to mix the iron water into the jars of dye, store the jars in the fridge and build a whole colour palette ready to use at a moment's notice.

You can make your own rust water and add a glug of this to each of your dyes or use a tiny sprinkle of ferrous sulphate (which is an iron salt) and watch the dye darken instantly. The acorn dye opposite was darkened with a tiny amount of ferrous sulphate and it immediately turned dark grey.

Make your own iron water

1. Fill a large glass jar with water.

2. Add pieces of iron and agitate every day or so. Open the jar and stir the contents to introduce oxygen, which is needed to form rust.

3. Keep adding more pieces of metal. The more metal you add, the more rust will form and the darker your jar of iron water will become.

4. To test your iron water, add a small amount of liquid to one of your tannin dyes and see if there is a change in colour. If not, then continue adding more metal, keep agitating and stir to add more oxygen and wait longer. You can also add vinegar to the jar as the acid will help with the formation of rust.

Storing dye

If you plan to dye your wood within the next 12-24 hours, then it will be fine sitting in the dye pot at room temperature. You could also put the dye pot outside with a lid on to keep it cooler (depending on your weather).

When painting wood with several colours of dye, I like to make all the dyes first and keep them in the fridge until I'm ready to paint. I store them in clean glass jars and clearly label them so no one will mistake them for food – they often look like sauces, so please be careful! You can also add salt to help preserve your dyes even better – just add a teaspoon of salt to the jar of dye and stir.

If you feel that the volume of liquid is too much, then simmer down the water to make it more concentrated. Avoid heating too aggressively as this can turn some dyes brown.

PREPARING THE DYE

Section 3

Dyeing beads, buttons & other small objects

- Pretreating wood with soya milk
- Dyeing wood in a dye bath
- Using iron to darken dyes

Pretreating wood with soya milk

If you have used soya milk to pretreat fabric in the past then you'll find this method similar. In fact the method for pretreating wood is even quicker since we don't need to spin out the excess milk from fabric – we just use a cloth to dry the surface of the wood.

The general principle is to soak our beads, buttons or other wooden items in very diluted soya milk for 12 hours, let the pieces dry fully, then soak in the diluted milk solution once or twice more.

Just like with fabric, we need to leave the beads for a few days before dyeing them. The main difference is that the milk is diluted even more than when we pretreat fabric. We are aiming for a very light and even coating of soy bean protein on the wood. If the milk isn't diluted enough and is too thick and creamy then it will leave an uneven coating on the wood which will cause an uneven colour later on.

You can either buy organic unsweetened soya milk from the supermarket or make your own soya milk by following the recipe on the next page.

Soak the wood in diluted milk

Very little milk is needed – a handful of wooden beads needs only a couple of tablespoons of milk diluted in water. I like to use any surplus milk to pretreat fabric in a separate bucket ready for dyeing. The method for fabric is detailed in my book *Botanical Colour at your Fingertips* (2016).

1. Soak your beads or small wooden items in a bowl of water for a couple of hours. The purpose of this is to open up the wood grain so the soya milk solution absorbs into the wood.

2. In a bowl, mix together 1 cup of water and 1 tablespoon of soya milk.

3. Put your beads or other wooden items into the bowl of diluted milk and stir well. It's best not to pack too many items into one bowl, so start a second bowl if in doubt.

4. Put the bowl in a cool place (even the fridge) and stir every few hours.

5. After 12 hours, strain the beads out of the milk and dry with a cloth and leave them to dry fully on a plate lined with another dry cloth.

6. In the meantime, keep the bowl of diluted milk in the fridge ready to use again when the beads are dry. If the milk is left out and curdles, mix another bowl of diluted milk with 1 tablespoon of soya milk and 1 cup of water.

7. When the beads are fully dry, pour them back into the bowl of diluted milk, stir for a minute or so, then strain out.

8. Dry them with a cloth and allow to dry on a plate lined with another dry cloth.

9. Wait a few days before dyeing the beads to allow the soy protein to cure and become part of the wood – a week is ideal.

Make soya milk

To make (just over) 250 ml soya milk you need:
30g organic soya beans
250ml water

1. Soak the soya beans in water overnight until they swell.

2. Put the beans and 250 ml water into a blender and blend until smooth.

3. Strain the milk through a muslin cloth or nut bag and squeeze in your hands. There will be pulp left in the muslin.

4. Add the pulp back into the blender with a little more fresh water and blend again.

5. Strain through a muslin cloth and pour the second lot of milk in with the first.

6. Repeat step 5 a couple more times and discard the last of the mushy soya bean bits.

Note: These instructions for raw soya milk are for craft/dyeing purposes only — as is everything in this book. To make soya milk for drinking, you need to follow particular processes (such as heating in a certain way), which is not covered here.

A few tips...

- Use very diluted milk so the layer of milk is even and not too thick.

- If you use supermarket milk, the concentration of milk may vary between brands. I use 1 cup of water mixed with 1 tablespoon of milk, but you may need to adjust this. Your first time doing this will be an experiment, so adjust the amounts accordingly the next time.

- Keep the bowl of milk somewhere cool so it stays fresh. You can even put the bowl of milk and beads in the fridge.

- Don't allow the milk to ferment. If the milk begins to curdle with the beads soaking in the bowl, it will leave a thick, patchy coating on the wood. This can sometimes be scraped off but often the beads are unlikely to dye a uniform colour.

- If the milk ferments, discard and mix up a new bowl of diluted milk. You only need 1 tablespoon of milk, so it's not much wastage if you need to discard some.

- A few thin coats in soya milk is much better than one coating in undiluted milk. Aim for a light coating so the layer of soy bean protein is applied evenly. A thick layer will just form a film over the surface that will peel off later and the wood will dye patchy.

- Experiment with other types of milk. It's the protein in soya beans that acts as a binder, so look at the protein content in other milk.

Dyeing wood in a dye bath

Now we will dye our beads, buttons or other small items in our dye pots. I often dye a range of items – some that have been treated in soya milk and some that have not. The pretreated beads will dye darker in the same dye pot, in comparison to the untreated beads. This produces a range of tones that work beautifully together within one design.

Layering different dyes can also be a useful tool for creating colour palettes and subtle effects. For example, take two dyes such as pomegranate skins and avocado skins and dye a handful of beads in each of these dyes. Then take a portion of each colour bead and dye them for a second time in the other dye pot to layer the colours. You will now have a range of tones that visually blend together.

← *Starting at the top moving clockwise, the dyes are: pomegranate skin (yellow dye), grey beads - eucalyptus modified with iron, lavender dye pot (tan colour), peach beads from avocado skins, yellow beads from pomegranate skins, a pot of avocado skin dye (dark pink).*

Dyeing in a dye bath

Achieving an even colour in the dye pot is fairly time intensive – you can't leave things unattended for long. So set some time aside to focus on your dye pots.

The size of your wooden items will determine the dye pot you use. For small beads and buttons, a small pot is ideal. For larger items you will need a deeper dye bath to cover your pieces, so a bigger pot is necessary.

1. Pour your dye into a small dye pot. For beads, you need a couple of inches of concentrated dye. For larger items, pour in enough to cover, plus some extra so there is enough depth so they can move around.

2. Heat to just below simmering point.

3. Very carefully – to avoid splashing hot liquid – drop your wooden items into the dye pot. Don't over pack the dye pot. It's best to dye fewer items and dye them evenly. For beads, only add in a single layer – when they float to the surface you want them all to be visible.

4. Beads will initially float, but as the dye permeates through the wood, they become full of water and usually sink. Larger items may continue to bob around the surface.

5. Keep stirring so they take the initial colour evenly. Heat very gently – below simmering point. We don't want to boil away the liquid or overheat the pot. Keep in mind that there is a risk that the wood will hit the bottom of the metal pot, singe and leave burn marks. Stir continually to keep everything moving.

DYEING BEADS, BUTTONS & OTHER SMALL OBJECTS

6. After about 15 minutes, turn off the heat and allow your wooden items to soak. Hopefully the beads will have sunk just below the surface by now and will stay submerged under dye. If they are still floating or if you are dyeing larger items which simply don't sink, then you can weigh the wood down with fabric. Add in damp fabric and push down so it absorbs the dye and holds the items below the surface. Our aim is keep the wood below the liquid at all times, but not right at the bottom of the pot as they may burn when coming into contact with the hot metal. The risk of burning is over once the pot cools.

7. Keep a close eye on your wooden items - don't leave the pot unattended for too long. You don't want any "tide mark" lines to form along the sides of the wood. This can happen when half is below the dye level and half is above. Set a timer for 5 or 10 minutes at a time and keep visiting your dye pot to give it a stir.

8. Observe how the wood is taking the dye. It's impossible to see the true colour when the wood is wet as it's naturally much darker. But can you see a difference between now and when the wood first got

wet? Decide if you would like to heat the dye again. Heat to just below simmering point and stir the beads for 5-10 minutes.

9. Allow the dye to cool and decide if you would like to remove your items at this point. If so, place your sieve over a bowl and strain into there. Then rinse the wooden items under the tap briefly and dry with a cloth. Allow them to dry on another dry cloth.

10. If you would like to keep dyeing for longer, either leave the items in the dye pot for longer or pour some of the dye into a glass jar and drop the items into the dye. Fill the jar almost to the top and make sure that all the beads or buttons are under the liquid level. Seal with a lid and leave on a sunny windowsill for a day or so. Shake the jar regularly to encourage everything to dye evenly. When you are ready, strain out of the dye, rinse under the tap, dry off on a cloth and allow to dry fully on a fresh cloth.

11. Leave the dye in your dye pot until your beads are fully dry. If you would like to dye them again for a darker colour then you can repeat the earlier steps.

DYEING BEADS, BUTTONS & OTHER SMALL OBJECTS

Using iron to darken dyes

I find it convenient to add iron water to some of my dyes and store the jars of dye in the fridge, so I have a small volume of several colours ready to use. This is especially handy when painting with dyes.

The grey dye, pictured opposite, was made from eucalyptus leaves with iron water added to shift the coral colour to grey. Follow the instructions in Section 2 to darken dyes with iron water. Then pour the darkened dye into a stainless steel saucepan and heat very gently. Never use an aluminium pan, as iron can contaminate it and all future dye baths will be darkened. Carefully add the beads into the dye bath and dye as usual. The wood will dye quicker than with non iron dyes, so adjust timings accordingly.

When working with iron, I always use a metal spoon and I reserve this spoon exclusively for iron dyes and label it. We must be careful, as iron can contaminate other dyes and accidentally darken colours. If you can, I suggest reserving a small dye pot just for iron dyeing. Even with a very thorough scrub, traces of iron can still affect the next dye that goes into the pot. I have a few inexpensive stainless steel pots that I use for dyeing beads – one of which is reserved for iron.

Ideally, get two sieves. I have one reserved for iron dyes and one for other dyes. Iron has a powerful effect on dyes so beware if your sieve is rusty. I've discoloured beads a few times in my rusty sieve and learnt not to leave beads sitting in there. I strain the liquid and pour out the beads immediately, otherwise the beads darken from contact with the metal.

← *Eucalyptus leaf dye darkened with iron to make grey dye.*

Section 4

Painting dye with a brush

- Painting flat surfaces
- Painting round beads
- Painting furniture

Painting flat surfaces

Concentrated dyes work on any kind of wood that has a porous surface. Unfinished wood is best but if you'd like to paint over a previously oiled or waxed surface, try sanding off the top layer so the dye can soak into the grain of the wood. Soya milk pretreatment isn't generally necessary as you can continue painting on more layers of dye until satisfied with the depth of colour. However the soy protein will help improve colour fastness of some dyes. To pretreat with milk, simply brush on layers of diluted milk and allow to dry between applications.

Several thin applications of dye are best. The mats in the photo opposite had three layers of dye. Wait until the previous coat is dry before painting on more dye. For an even finish, paint in the same direction as the grain. You may choose to lightly sand the wood between dye applications if the grain opens up and becomes rough.

The possibilities are endless. You can use dye to tint an entire surface or create intricate artworks on wood. Each piece will be unique since the grain of the wood is always visible through dye. The potential for creating paintings on wood with these botanical dyes is exciting – you're only limited by your imagination. I'm not a painter so I tend to stick to creating simple patterns, but don't let this stop you taking things further! Light fastness is an important consideration for artwork, so refer to Section 5.

acorn dye +
ferrous sulphate

PAINTING DYE WITH A BRUSH

BOTANICAL DYES ON WOOD

Painting round beads

Dyes can be applied to beads in the same way as flat surfaces. The only difference is that beads are usually curved which means we must apply thinner layers of dye as the liquid can easily drip down the curved side.

You may find it helpful to carefully thread your beads onto a stick or skewer so you don't smudge the dye as you're painting. If you don't have a stick that's the right width to fit snugly into the hole, you can just hold one very carefully in your fingers. I usually do the latter then stand them upright to dry, with the hole at the bottom.

Very light applications of dye work best on beads, so the liquid is less likely to run and spoil the outline of the pattern you're creating. To make stripes, paint in the same direction as the wood grain. For dots, apply little droplets of dye so they spread out into larger spots. Always test your ideas on a sample bead before painting a whole collection.

For the patterned beads pictured opposite, I painted five layers of dye and waited about half an hour between coats, so the previous layer had soaked in and was touch-dry. This may seem time-intensive, but I simply left the beads on a windowsill and popped back for a few minutes throughout the day to apply subsequent layers of dye.

Painting furniture

Botanical dyes work beautifully on larger expanses of wood too. The dyes tint the wood and allow the grain to show. This mini chest of drawers (from IKEA) is an example of what you could create. Here, the smooth, unfinished plywood has absorbed the dye well. Three applications of dye were used to achieve this depth of colour. So long as the surface of the wood is unfinished, try painting an inconspicuous area first, such as the back or inside a drawer to see how the dye absorbs. If you're happy with the result, then paint the entire piece. The dyes I chose to use here are all fairly colour fast which is an important consideration for furniture.

1. Make your dyes and store them in jars in the fridge ready for painting. Add iron to the dyes as needed and label them all.
2. Using a clean brush for each jar of dye, paint the dyes onto the wood in the direction of the grain. Apply the dye in thin layers and work quickly so the liquid spreads across the surfaces evenly.
3. Leave to dry fully before applying a second layer of dye.
4. Repeat for a third layer of dye and continue layering to achieve the depth of colour you would like.
5. Decide if you will coat with a sealant such as oil or glue. (Section 5 outlines the pros and cons of each).

Top drawers: yellow (pomegranate skin), pink (avocado skin).
Middle drawers: purple (avocado skin + iron), caramel (alder cone).
Bottom drawers: pink (avocado skin), grey (eucalyptus leaves + iron).

PAINTING DYE WITH A BRUSH

Section 5

Aftercare

- Oiling wood
- Other sealants
- Colour fastness

BOTANICAL DYES ON WOOD

Oiling wood

Once your dyed or painted wood is fully dry, you may choose to apply a coating of oil. Oiling is beneficial because it:

- seals in the colour.
- nourishes the wood and prevents it from drying out and potentially cracking.
- gives the wood a lovely sheen.
- darkens the colour – you can even play around with oiling some beads and not oiling others to get different effects.

My favourite wood oil is linseed oil. I have a bottle of cold pressed organic linseed oil that I keep in the fridge. I only use a tiny bit at a time so it's very economical.

To oil beads, pour some linseed oil onto a rag and simply rub it onto the beads one by one. Then place the beads onto a plate and leave them there for a day so any excess oil can absorb. This step is important as we don't want our clothes to get stained from a freshly oiled necklace! When you're happy that the wood has absorbed the oil, either use them for whatever you had in mind or store for later.

To oil flat surfaces, simply rub an oil soaked cloth in the same direction as the wood grain. Apply a second coat if desired.

Other sealants

Another option for sealing wood is to apply a layer of water-based glue. Unlike oil, glue doesn't darken dyes. Applying oil over dyed wood usually alters colours slightly – greys become slightly brown. If you're creating artwork and don't want to darken your colours, then you could apply a water-based glue over your work. The white glue dries transparent.

In the photo opposite, the three mats on the left have been painted with *Mod Podge* (matte) and the six other mats have been coated in linseed oil.

Always test on a sample piece or hidden area before painting over a larger surface to check that it gives you the finish you're looking for.

Glue doesn't nourish the wood like oil does, so the finished piece may be rough to the touch. This could be fine for artwork to be hung and not touched, but has its downsides for more tactile items. Keep this in mind when deciding. Also, once painted with glue, you can't apply oil at a later date to nourish the wood as it won't absorb through the glue. The glue doesn't enhance patterns in the wood grain, which can have its advantages, if that's the finish you're looking for.

Oiling is my favourite way to seal wood, but glue is still a useful alternative with the distinct advantage of not darkening colours.

AFTERCARE

73

BOTANICAL DYES ON WOOD

Colour fastness

How well do the colours last? There are three elements of colour fastness that we can test:

1. **Light fastness** is most applicable for items left out in the light such as furniture, artwork and jewellery. It's important to use light fast dyes for these.
2. **Wash fastness** is most important to check when dyeing buttons for clothing that will be washed.
3. **Rub fastness** must be checked when dyeing beads to ensure that the colour doesn't rub onto clothing.

1. Light fastness

To test the light fastness of beads, leave a bead out in the light for a few weeks and compare to one that has been kept in the dark. Is there much fading? If so, then take note of this and don't use this plant if selling dyed items, as these colours need to last. For gifts, maybe you can offer to redye if the colour fades or tell friends how to dye them again.

If you're planning to paint a piece of furniture or make some artwork, it's important to do a test on a small piece of wood first. Cover half with a piece of cardboard and leave out in the light and see how much fading there is after a few weeks.

2. Wash fastness

This is not much of an issue for necklaces, but a good degree of wash fastness is important for buttons that will be washed on clothing. To test for colour loss and transfer, sew a button onto a swatch of light fabric and wash a few times and see if the colour transfers onto the fabric or if the button fades compared to an unwashed button. Use these tests to decide which dyes are most suited to buttons. My preference is to dye buttons with a tannin dye and iron for the best level of wash fastness.

3. Rub fastness

Sometimes very dark beads and buttons can rub their dye onto fabric. All dyed wood may transfer dye onto a surface if rubbed very hard, but a well dyed bead or button shouldn't rub its colour onto fabric when worn. Sometimes very dark beads need an extra rinse at the end of the dyeing process to remove the excess dye. Then when they are dry, they can be oiled to help seal in the colour and prevent any colour transfer.

Before committing to dyeing a large batch of beads for necklaces, first test the rub fastness of the dye. If colour transfers, try rinsing the beads more thoroughly to remove any unattached dye particles. There may simply be too much dye on the surface of the bead and this needs to be removed. Let the bead dry and oil it. Allow the oil to soak in fully and test the rub fastness of the bead again.

Section 6

Appendix

- Painting paper & fabric
- Pretreating fabric in soya milk
- Hammering flowers onto wood
- Glossary
- UK - US vocabulary differences
- Bibliography
- About Rebecca Desnos

BOTANICAL DYES ON WOOD

Painting paper & fabric

If you've followed the steps in this book and dyed with a range of plants, by now you may find that you have quite a collection of dye in your fridge! When you've dyed or painted all the wood you planned, you may wonder what else can you use these dyes for.

These concentrated dyes are an ideal consistency for painting anything you like. They work beautifully on fabric or as watercolours on paper. You can use dyes in their current state, which is my preference, as I love the flow of the water, or you can thicken them into more of a paste with a range of gums, yogurt or flour.

Dyes as watercolour paints

The photo opposite shows goldenrod dye that I made in an aluminium pot with a minimal amount of water, like we do with all the dyes in this book. I used just enough water to cover the flowers to make the dye as concentrated as possible. The yellow dye shifted to green in the pot and made a wonderful watercolour paint. The orange splashes on the far left are from a very strong cup of rooibos tea.

Make your own watercolour paints with any kind of concentrated dye. Follow the storage instructions in Section 2 and keep them in the fridge.

Painting fabric

Concentrated dyes also work beautifully on fabric. You can either use them in their original watery consistency or thicken them with a range of powdered gums or even mix with a small amount of yogurt to form a paste. In the photo opposite, I thickened the dyes with a tiny amount of gum tragacanth which increases the viscosity of the dye slightly. This stops the dye bleeding out into the fibres and enables us to apply the dye with more precision.

How to thicken dyes

What you need:

Concentrated dye (method in Section 2).
Gum tragacanth (order online from cake decorating or herbal stores).
Small saucepan, whisk or fork, glass jar, paint brush.

1. Wash your fabric then pretreat in soya milk following the method on page 84. Wait a week before painting or dyeing to allow the protein to cure on the fibres.
2. Pour approximately half a cup of dye into a small saucepan and begin to heat gently, but do not boil. As the liquid heats up, sprinkle half a teaspoon of powdered gum tragacanth and whisk thoroughly. It will thicken further as it cools.
3. Paint your fabric and store any left over paint in a jar in the fridge. Label clearly so it's not mistaken for food.
4. Allow the fabric to dry naturally, then iron with high heat to set the dye. Wait at least a week before rinsing out the excess dye.

Dyes made from: pomegranate skins (yellow), avocado stones (dark red), black tea (brown).

APPENDIX

Pretreating fabric in soya milk

Soya (soy) milk can be used as a pretreatment on fabric, acting as a binding agent between plant fibres and plant dyes. The soy protein binds to cellulose fibres, making them more receptive to plant dyes. This improves colourfastness and helps achieve darker dye colours.

The following recipe pretreats up to 400g of fabric. Buy soya milk that contains as few additives as possible. The following method uses store bought milk; homemade soya milk is more concentrated so will need to be diluted further. The aim is to coat the fibres with several layers of diluted milk – a thick layer will lead to uneven dyeing results later on.

Try to do this on a cool day so the milk stays as fresh as possible. Discard the milk if it curdles. This is a summary of the method in *Botanical Colour at your Fingertips* (2016).

← To make soya milk from dried beans, follow the recipe on page 49.

Soya milk method

1. Pour 1 litre of soya milk into a bucket and add 5 litres of water. Add your clean fabric in there and mix well. If the fabric isn't fully submerged, add more water. Leave to soak for 12 hours.

2. Remove fabric, then squeeze out the milk. Spin out the excess liquid in the washing machine (spin cycle with no water). Hang to dry.

3. Dip the fabric in the bucket of milk again to receive an even coating, squeeze by hand, then spin out the excess in the washing machine. Allow to dry.

4. Do a final dip in the milk, squeeze out, then spin out in the washing machine. Use a quick wash cycle to clean your empty machine.

5. Leave the fabric to dry then set aside for a week before painting or dyeing, so the soy protein can cure on the fabric.

Hammering flowers onto wood

Imagine making realistic plant prints on wood. Yes, that really is possible! I show you how to do this in my *Plant Dye Zine,* which is available in print or as an eBook. Pop over to *rebeccadesnos.com* to order a copy.

Essentially, you lay flowers or leaves face down onto wood, cover with a piece of fabric and begin hammering. In the zine, I take you through the process step by step and share some tips with you. I give detailed instructions for making and decorating a flower press, or you could create beautiful artwork for the wall.

APPENDIX

Glossary

cellulose fibre. A fibre of plant origin such as cotton, linen, hemp or wood.

colour fastness. To assess the colour fastness of dyed fibres, we consider the combined results from light, wash and rub fastness tests.

dyestuff. A substance used to dye fibres. In this book 'whole dyestuff' refers to plants that are used to dye wood

fugitive dye. Dyes that eventually fade despite mordanting, e.g. beetroot, tumeric and hibiscus flowers.

iron water. Water that contains tiny particles of rust – also known as rust water. Iron water can be added to dyes to darken the colours.

light fastness. The degree to which a dyed material maintains colour through exposure to sunlight.

mordant. A substance used to fix dye to fibres. In this book, the mordants used are tannins, aluminium dye pots and iron water. Soya milk is technically a binder but for simplicity it is sometimes referred to as a mordant.

rub fastness. The degree to which colour transfers from a dyed material to another surface through the action of rubbing.

tannins. Naturally occurring compounds found in seeds, leaves, bark and fruit. Tannins play an important role in plant dyeing and act as natural mordants and fix dyes to fibres.

wash fastness. The degree to which a dyed material maintains colour through repeated washing.

wood dye. A dye permeates into the layers of the wood and bonds with fibres. The wood grain is still visible – the dye appears as a translucent wash of colour.

wood stain. A wood stain sits on the surface and is usually within an oil based medium.

UK – US vocabulary differences

UK English has been used throughout this book, so US readers may notice a few spelling differences. Below are a handful of words translated for clarity.

avocado stones	-	avocado seeds or pits
bicarbonate of soda	-	baking soda
soya milk	-	soy milk

APPENDIX

Bibliography

DEAN, Jenny. 2010. *Wild Colour. How to grow, prepare and use natural plant dyes.* Octopus Publishing Group.

DESNOS, Rebecca. 2016. *Botanical Colour at your Fingertips.* Published by Rebecca Desnos.

DESNOS, Rebecca (and other contributors). 2020. *Plant Dye Zine.* Published by Rebecca Desnos.

FLINT, India. 2008. *Eco Colour. Botanical dyes for beautiful textiles.* Murdoch Books.

JOHNSTON, Ann. 2001. *Color by Design. Paint and Print with Dye.* Published by Ann Johnston.

LOGAN, Jason. 2018. *Make Ink. A Forager's Guide to Natural Inkmaking.* Abrams.

NEDDO, Nick. 2015. *The Organic Artist.* Quarry Books.

Rebecca dip dyeing cotton in avocado dye

About Rebecca Desnos

Rebecca Desnos is a natural dyer, writer and independent publisher who lives in England. Her passion lies in sharing her surprisingly simple methods and empowering others to try new things. Well known on Instagram for dyeing with avocados, Rebecca shares her experiments with thousands of crafters all over the world.

Rebecca has a varied background in linguistics and interior design, and has been a crafter since her childhood. Now, as a mother, she finds that plant dyeing is the perfect antidote to busy life. She fills her bag with plants wherever she goes, always in search of new colours.

Rebecca released her first book, *Botanical Colour at your Fingertips,* in 2016. Rebecca's latest book is called *Plant Dye Zine* (2020): learn how to make paint and ink, bundle dye with flowers, eco-print with leaves, start a dye garden and lots more.

For more dyeing tutorials, visit **rebeccadesnos.com**
Follow Rebecca on Instagram **@rebeccadesnos**

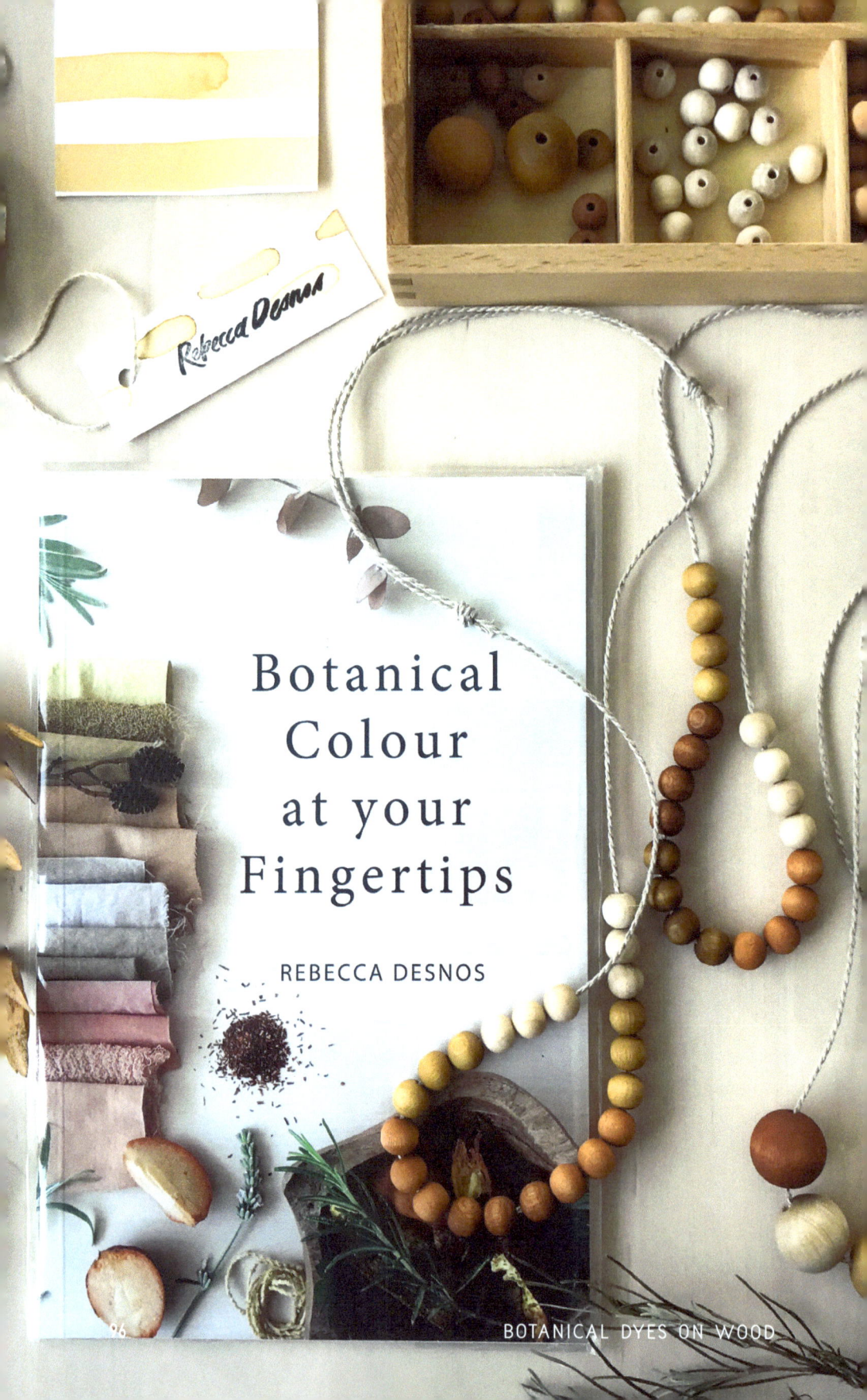

96 | BOTANICAL DYES ON WOOD

Enjoy your dyeing!

Thank you for buying *Botanical Dyes on Wood* and supporting my work! I hope this book has brought you joy and you will go on to experiment with plant dyes.

If you'd like to learn more about dyeing fabric and yarn, my first book *Botanical Colour at your Fingertips* guides you through my process step-by-step and will give you the confidence to get started.

I'd love to keep in touch with you! Please tag me in any projects you share on Instagram with the hashtag #rebeccadesnos.

If you'd like to hear more from me, then you're welcome to join my newsletter on my website: *rebeccadesnos.com/newsletter*

Rebecca

Notes...

www.ingramcontent.com/pod-product-compliance
Lightning Source LLC
Chambersburg PA
CBHW041508010526
44118CB00006B/188